"QUOTES for Kids"

WORDS FOR KIDS TO LIVE BY

Compiled by Katura J. Hudson

Illustrations by Howard Simpson

Just Us BOOKS

AFRO-BETS ® Quotes for Kids:
Words for Kids to Live By

Copyright 1999 by Just Us Books, Inc.

Text compiled by Katura J. Hudson
Illustrations and design by Howard Simpson

Inquiries should be addressed to:
JUST US BOOKS, INC.
356 Glenwood Avenue
East Orange, NJ 07017
www.justusbooks.com

Printed in Canada/First Edition 10 9 8 7 6 5 4 3 2 1

Cataloging-in-Publication data is available.

ISBN: 0-940975-89-0

Contents

Learning from the Animals

By going and coming, a bird weaves its nest.

-- *Ashanti proverb*

Let the elephant fell the trees,
Let the bushpig dig the holes,
Let the mason wasp fill in the walls,
Let the giraffe put up the roof,
Then we'll have a house.

-- *Zaire*

When spider webs unite, they can tie up a lion.

-- Ethiopian proverb

Don't lay it on the cow when the milk goes sour.

-- Traditional

When the mouse laughs at the cat,
there is a hole nearby.

-- Nigerian proverb

Do not be like the mosquito that bites
the owner of the house.

-- Liberian proverb

The monkey does not see his own hind parts; he sees his neighbors'.

-- Zimbabwean proverb

Rooster makes more racket than the hen that lays the egg.

-- Guinea proverb

No elephant ever found its trunk
too heavy.

-- Zulu

The monkey, having one day eaten too
much, desires that his fore-teeth
be drawn.

-- Yoruba

The dog has four feet, but he does not walk them in four roads.

By trying often, the monkey learns to jump from the tree.

The slowest camel in the caravan sets the pace.

-- Somalia

A cow that has no tail should not try to chase away flies.

-- Guinea proverb

It's nothing to lead the snake to school.
Making it sit down is the hard part.

-- Haitian proverb

Some birds avoid the water.
Ducks seek it.

-- Nigerian proverb

Afro-mation

Animals have much to teach us.
We must take the time to learn
from them.

-- Langston

Listening to
the Elders

The small child looks everywhere and sees nought; but the old man sitting on the ground sees everything.

-- Senegal

The situation of our youth is not mysterious. Children have never been very good at listening to their elders, but they have never failed to imitate them.

-- James Baldwin 1961

Let's not get too full of ourselves.
Let's leave space for God to come into
the room.

-- Quincy Jones

The way to make a mountain out of a
molehill is to keep on adding dirt.

-- Anonymous

In every difficulty you can find
an opportunity.

-- Traditional

You can't hold a man down without staying
down with him.

-- attributed to Booker T. Washington

If there is no struggle there is no progress.

-- Frederick Douglass

Trust in the Lord with all thine heart;
and lean not unto thine own under-
standing. In all thy ways acknowledge
Him, and He shall direct thy paths.

-- Proverbs 3: 5-6

When your hand is in leopard's mouth,
be careful how you pull it out.

-- Liberia

I learned that no matter what you may
or may not have, as perceived by a
misguided community about what is
valuable, people understand hard work
and talent - and it can prevail.

-- Maxine Waters

The man who views the world at fifty
the same as he did at twenty has
wasted thirty years of his life.

-- Muhammad Ali

The one being carried does not realize
how far away the town is.

-- Nigerian proverb

If you don't have the best of everything,
make the best of everything you have.

-- Anonymous

The fruit must have a stem before it grows.

-- Jabo proverb (Liberia)

A blind man may hear more
than you see.

-- South Africa

Give some people an inch and they
think they're a ruler.

-- Anonymous

Afro-mation

Grandma likes to tell stories about the old days. I like to listen, too, because I learn about my family and my history.

-- Glo

Believing
in
Yourself

I have learned that success is to be measured not so much by the position that one has reached in life as by the obstacles which one has to overcome while trying to succeed.

-- Booker T. Washington

I am/I can.

-- Graffiti in Harlem

If you have no confidence in self, you are twice defeated in the race of life. With confidence, you have won even before you have started.

-- Marcus Garvey

I used to want the words "She tried" on my tombstone. Now I want "She did it."

-- Katherine Dunham

A man can get along if he has faith in the goodness of other people ...and believes in himself.

-- Roy Wilkins

I'm a cute little girl with a cute little figure, But step back, stay 'way, boys, 'til I get a little bigger.

-- playground rhyme

I don't think I was courageous. I think I was determined.

-- Daisy Bates

The most important challenge in my life is to always test the limits of my abilities, do the best job I can at the time while remaining true to myself.

-- Dr. Mae C. Jemison

I can accept failure.
Everyone fails at something.
But I cannot accept not trying.

-- Michael Jordan, "I Can't Accept Not Trying" 1994

Never accept the negative thought, "I can't make it because I'm black." You can't concede defeat before you even start.

-- James Earl Jones

Detest anything less than doing
your best.

-- overheard at the Million Man March

We are troubled on every side, yet not
distressed; we are perplexed, but not in
despair; persecuted, but not forsaken;
cast down, but not destroyed.

-- II Corinthians 4:8-9

To be a great champion you must believe you are the best. If you're not, pretend you are.

-- Muhammad Ali

Excellence is to do a common thing in an uncommon way.

-- Booker T. Washington

The human being is transformed by
where his mind goes,
not where his body goes.

-- Naíim Akbar

God works in me to will and to do
whatever he wishes me to do. God
cannot fail. Therefore I cannot fail.

-- written in a private journal

Afro-mation

> I know I can do it!
> I know I can do it!
> Believing that is the first step
> in accomplishing my goal.

> -- Stef

Being a
Good Friend

A man that hath friends must shew himself friendly; and there is a friend that sticketh closer than a brother.

-- Proverbs 18:24

To give to thy friend is not to cast away, it is to store for the future.

-- Swahili

The friends of our friends
are our friends.

-- Congolese folk saying

One man you can trust is better than
an army of cowards.

-- Egypt

Equals make the best friends.

-- Aesop, "The Two Pots"

Do unto others as you would have
them do unto you.

-- Golden rule

Friendship that is kept up only while
eyes see does not go to the heart.

-- Yoruba

Iron sharpeneth iron; so a man
sharpeneth the countenance of his friend.

-- Proverbs 27:17

An enemy slaughters, a friend distributes.

-- Fulfulde proverb

Help others and you help yourself.

-- Dave Dinwiddie, "My Father"

Love your neighbor as you love yourself.

-- Luke 10:27

A good friend is one who praises you
when you're not there.

-- Yoruba

Friendship can neither
be bought nor sold.

-- Morocco

You give little when you give of your
possessions. It is when you give of
yourself that you truly give.

-- Khalil Gibran

We are inevitably our brother's keeper because we are our brother's brother.

-- Dr. Martin Luther King, Jr.
"Where Do We Go From Here: Chaos or Community?"

Friend! It is a common word, often lightly used. Like other good and beautiful things, it may be tarnished by careless handling.

-- Harriet Jacobs,
"Incidents in the Life of a Slave Girl"

Afro-mation

> If you want to have a friend,
> You must be a friend.
>
> -- Nandi

Planning
for the
Future

The issue is no longer where you sit on the bus or whether you can drive it; it's whether you can develop the capital to own the bus company.

-- William H. Gray III

There is no reason to repeat bad history.

-- Eleanor Holmes Norton

If you do not know where you are going, any road will take you there.

-- Anonymous

A lazy man will wait 'til easy work comes his way.

-- Traditional

It is quite easy to shout slogans, to sign manifestos, but it is quite a different matter to build, manage, command, spend days and nights seeking the solution of problems.

-- Patrice Lumumba

The best time to do a thing is when it can be done.

-- William Pickens

Where there is a road,
people have passed before.

-- Kimbundu

While I was sleeping in my bed there,
things were happening in the world
that directly concerned me - nobody
asked me, consulted me - they just
went out and did things, and changed
my life.

-- Lorraine Hansberry
"Raisin in the Sun"

Yesterday can take care of itself.

-- Traditional

You're either part of the solution or you're part of the problem.

-- attributed to Eldridge Cleaver

Don't forget where you came from.

-- Anonymous

Some people are your relatives but others are your ancestors, and you choose the ones you want to have as ancestors. You create yourself out of those values.

-- Ralph Ellison

While the sun shines, get firewood for the night.

-- Zambia

I don't want you to praise me ... Some praise me because I am a colored girl and I don't want that kind of praise. I had rather you would point out my defects, for that will teach me something.

-- Edmonia Lewis

Many people worry, but they don't do anything about it.

-- Pearl Bailey

Do not look where you fell, but where you slipped.

-- Vai

Afro-mation

*To have a successful future, I know
I must prepare for it.*

--Robo

Building a
Better World

We must not, in trying to think about
how we can make a big difference
ignore the small daily differences we
can make, which over time,
add up to big differences that we often
cannot foresee.

-- Marian Wright Edelman

Count your blessings -- not your troubles.

-- Traditional

We must find an alternative
to violence. The eye for an eye
philosophy leaves everybody blind.

-- Dr. Martin Luther King,

No race can prosper 'til it learns that
there is as much dignity in tilling a field
as in writing a poem.

-- Booker T. Washington

The weak can never forgive. Forgiveness is the attribute of the strong.

-- Mahatma Gandhi

Before healing others, heal thyself.

-- Wolof proverb

The price of hating other human beings is loving oneself less.

-- Eldridge Cleaver

If people around you aren't going any-where, if their dreams are no bigger than hanging out on the corner or they're dragging you down, get rid of them. Negative people can sap your energy so fast and they can take your dreams from you, too.

-- Magic Johnson

Starting a war is easy. Ending it is not.

-- Egypt

It's hard to talk about yourself all day...
You learn when you're with other
ideas, other books, other friends.
Talking about yourself can't advance
your life.

-- Yannick Noah

It is not enough to learn the truth
unless you also learn to live it.

-- Traditional

Nobody can do everything,
but everybody can do something,
and if everybody does something,
everything will get done.

-- Gil Scott Heron

Doing what's right today means no regrets tomorrow.

-- Anonymous

Remember to forgive -- then remember to forget.

-- Source Unknown

Our purpose on earth is not to get used to the dark, but to shine as lights.

-- The Daily Word

As we have opportunity,
let us do good to all.

-- Galatians 6:10

Afro-mation

> I lend a hand wherever I can. I'm helping to make a better world.
>
> -- Tura

Acknowledgments

Katura J. Hudson
compiler

Katura J. Hudson earned her B.A. in American Studies from Douglass College, Rutgers University in 1998. A native of East Orange, New Jersey, she is a media relations coordinator for a major foundation headquartered in New York City. This is her first published book.

Howard Simpson
illustrator and designer

Born and raised in Newark, New Jersey, **Howard Simpson** began his art career by drawing storyboards for Action News and Accu Weather while studying at Temple University's Tyler School of Art. He lives in New Jersey with his wife and children.

The Quotations

The quotes listed in this book come from a variety of sources and the oral tradition of African American public speaking. Traditional sayings are attributed to various regions, languages or ethnic groups on the continent of Africa, ie. Vai, Liberia, Yoruba, Swahili, Morocco, etc. Many of the individuals quoted are contemporary public figures or notable persons in African American culture. Wherever possible the editor has noted the exact context of the quotations and gratefully acknowledges these sources.